games pe●ple play!

Mexico

R. Conrad Stein

CHILDRENS PRESS®

CHICAGO

Editorial Staff

Project Editor: Mark Friedman

Photo Research: Feldman & Associates

Fact Checker: Dana Burnell

Design Staff

Design and Electronic Composition:
TJS Design

Maps: TJS Design

Cover Art and Icons: Susan Kwas

Activity Page Art: MacArt Design

Editorial Consultants

George I. Blanksten, Ph.D.
Northwestern University
Evanston, Illinois

D. Donne Bryant

Library of Congress Cataloging-in-Publication Data

Stein, R. Conrad
Mexico / by R. Conrad Stein.
p. cm.—(Games people play)
Summary: Describes various games and sports played in Mexico, including soccer, boxing, and bullfighting.
ISBN 0-516-04439-7
1. Sports—Mexico—Juvenile literature. 2. Sports—Mexico—Sociological aspects—Juvenile literature. 3. Athletes—Mexico—Biography—Juvenile literature. [1. Sports—Mexico.] I. Title. II. Series

GV587.S74 1995   95-2701
796'.0972—dc20   CIP
                                    AC

Mexican boys and girls
playing "sea serpent"

Table of Contents

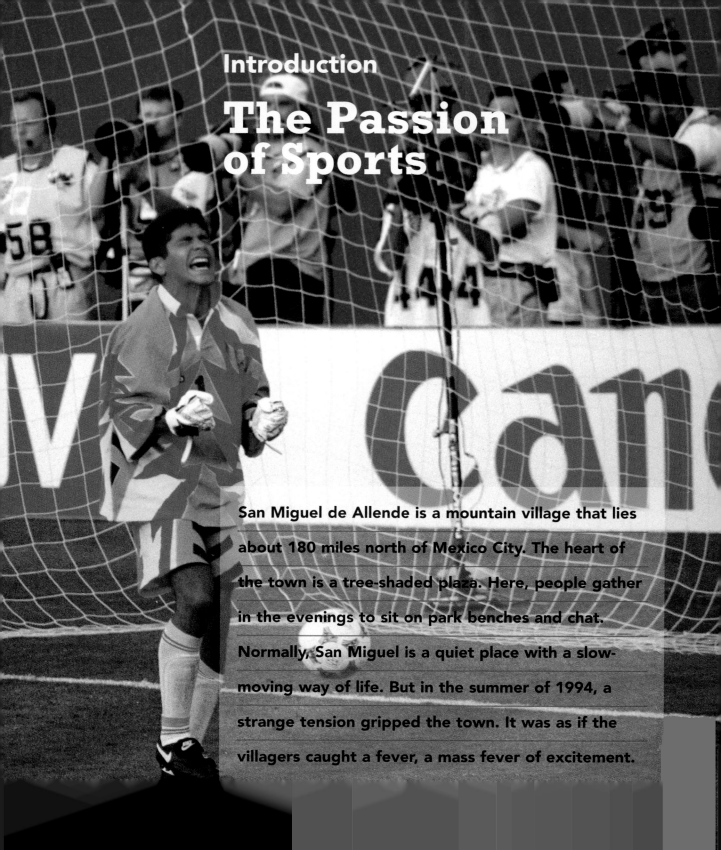

The Passion of Sports

San Miguel de Allende is a mountain village that lies about 180 miles north of Mexico City. The heart of the town is a tree-shaded plaza. Here, people gather in the evenings to sit on park benches and chat. Normally, San Miguel is a quiet place with a slow-moving way of life. But in the summer of 1994, a strange tension gripped the town. It was as if the villagers caught a fever, a mass fever of excitement.

Mexican fans rally outside Giants Stadium in New Jersey on the day of Mexico's big World Cup game in 1994.

¡Los mejores, aqui estamos! ¡México! ¡México!

San Miguel, like the rest of Mexico, was in a frenzy over the Mexican soccer team, which had advanced to the second round in the World Cup competition. Held once every four years, the World Cup is the "World Series" of soccer.

Finally the day of the big game arrives. Children proudly display trading cards bearing pictures of star players. Men discuss soccer strategy in cafes. High school students jam the plaza, singing a haunting song: "¡Los mejores, aqui estamos! ¡México! ¡México!..." (The best, here we are! Mexico! Mexico!)

A collision between a Mexican (green jersey) and Bulgarian player in the 1994 World Cup

The game pits Mexico against Bulgaria. Bulgaria is a team *muy fuerte* (very strong), one of the best squads in Europe. The game is played at Giants Stadium near New York City and is televised live to Mexico. When the game begins, San Miguel's streets are deserted. No one walks about. Few cars are seen. All of the town's residents sit at home or in restaurants to catch every breathless minute of the action on television.

The two teams duel back and forth, back and forth, over the field. Suddenly, a goal. Mexico scores a goal! A great roar explodes in every room in San Miguel where people are watching the game. But the Bulgarian team quickly responds by scoring a goal of its own. Throughout town, an anxious sigh is heard.

At the end of regulation play, the score is tied, 1 to 1. The two teams begin a sudden-death overtime period. The first team to score will win. And then, a strange phenomenon begins in San

Miguel. One by one and in family groups, people go up to their roofs to pray. The rooftops of village houses are flat, and families often hang their wash there. Now they climb to the roofs to be closer to God. Some drop to their knees; others simply bow their heads. All pray for victory.

When the gun sounds ending the overtime period, neither team has scored. The contest will now be decided by a shootout. Each team will have five free kicks at the opponent's goal. Only the goalie is allowed to block the shots. Mexican fans know the Bulgarians are stronger kickers than the Mexicans. And sure enough, the Bulgarians' kicks thunder into the Mexican net. The Mexican team is defeated.

In San Miguel, fans pour out onto the streets. Once more, students crowd into the plaza. Many have tears in their eyes.

Yet they wave the Mexican flag and shout, *"¡Viva México!"* Never before had the Mexican national team advanced as far as the second round in World Cup competition. This team, though it lost a game, is still a winner. People cheer themselves hoarse. Cars honk their horns furiously. And the students sing: *"¡Los mejores, aqui estamos! ¡México! ¡México!"*

Mexican players were devastated after losing in the World Cup, but Mexican fans still celebrated them as heroes.

Mexico at a Glance

Land

Mexico's area is approximately 760,000 square miles, counting its outlying islands. It is bordered by the Pacific Ocean to the west, the Gulf of Mexico to the east, and the Caribbean Sea to the southeast, making for 6,320 miles of coastline. Mexico City is the capital and the largest city.

People

In 1994, Mexico's population was estimated at nearly 92 million. Mexico City's population was 19.5 million. Most people in Mexico speak Spanish as their primary language. But many English words are used frequently in Mexico, just as many Spanish words are used frequently in the United States. Several Indian languages (such as Maya, Mixtec, and Zapotec) are also used by the country's more than five million Indians. Nearly all Mexicans (97 percent of the population) belong to the Roman Catholic Church.

Government

Mexico's official name is *Los Estados Unidos de México* (the United States of Mexico). Like the United States of America, it is a federation of states held together by a central government. Mexico is divided into 31 states and one federal district. The federal district contains its capital, Mexico City. Mexico's president serves one six-year term and is then not allowed to be re-elected. The Mexican Congress has two houses—the Chamber of Deputies and the Senate.

History

Great civilizations such as the Maya and Aztec rose in Mexico in pre-Hispanic times. Spain conquered the country in the 1520s and ushered in three centuries of Spanish rule. The Mexican people fought a War of Independence from 1810 to 1820 and freed themselves from Spain. War with the United States (1846-48) cost Mexico its vast northern territories. Today, these territories comprise California, Arizona, New Mexico, Nevada, Utah, and parts of Wyoming and Colorado. A Mexican civil war fought from 1910 to 1920 resulted in tremendous damage and loss of life. Since 1920, Mexico has enjoyed peace. Though large-scale poverty still exists, the growth of factories in the 1980s and 1990s brought Mexico more industrial jobs than ever before in its history.

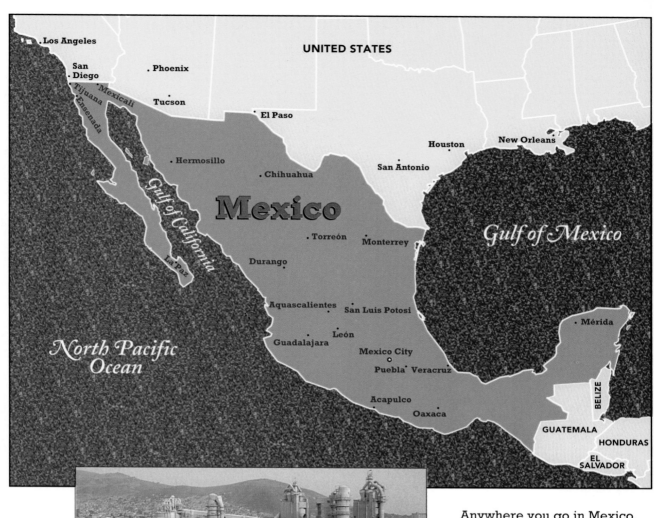

Anywhere you go in Mexico, it's not hard to find children playing soccer. The soccer field shown here is in the heart of Mexico City.

Art, music, and literature are passions in Mexico.

Mexico is a land where a singer will unashamedly

shed a tear when singing a sad ballad. A Mexican

poet, reciting his work in a coffeehouse, will

clench his fists and shout the lines to the heavens.

So it is understandable that the energy of sports

also seizes the Mexican soul.

In the early 1500s, Spanish soldiers were astounded when they marched into central Mexico and discovered the Aztec capital city, Tenochtitlán, rising like a great jewel in the mountains.

The Spaniards marveled at its broad streets, opulent palaces, and mighty pyramids piercing the sky. Nowhere in Europe was there a larger or more splendid city.

The Spaniards also discovered that the Aztecs were devoted to sports and games. They gambled wildly on a board game that was played with dice. Entire villages watched and people cheered while nimble-footed boys participated in **pole-climbing** contests, scrambling to the top like monkeys.

The Aztecs' favorite team sport was **_tlatchtli_** (pronounced TLASH-tli), which resembled soccer and basketball combined. When playing tlachtli, two teams advanced a hard, rubber ball using their elbows, knees, and hips. The object was to propel the ball through a vertical ring about 18 inches in diameter. Tlachtli was more than one

Modern-day Mexican Indians re-create the ancient pole-climbing ritual.

Ancient Indians play a ball game that is similar to today's basketball (above); at the Xochicalco archeological site, a centuries-old ball court still exists (top).

thousand years old even before the Spaniards arrived. A similar game was the favorite sport of the ancient Maya people who lived south of the Aztec empire. The Maya played on an I-shaped court with a large, rubber ball. Goals were scored when a team pushed the ball into the opposing team's end zone, much like modern soccer. To the Maya, the game was a religious exercise, and they added a grim twist to the outcome. As a sacrifice to the gods, the captain of the winning team was sometimes allowed to cut off the head of the losing team's captain.

Just like children around the world, Mexican children love soccer, and they play it any time and anywhere.

fútbol

The Spanish term for "soccer"

In modern Mexico, people play **soccer** with the same kind of intensity as their ancestors. But now the losing coach goes home minus only his pride—not his head. The thrill of soccer *(fútbol)* envelops the nation. Boys and girls begin kicking soccer balls when they are only two or three years old. Pickup games take place in rocky fields where a pair of cactuses serve as goalposts. Grade schools and high schools sponsor teams. Villages play other villages, and rivalries are ferocious.

Players for the Mexico City
Cruz Azul soccer team
(blue jerseys)

The pride of the Mexican soccer scene is the pro league, a collection of teams manned by the nation's best players. Pro games are televised throughout the country, and they can also be seen on Spanish-language channels in the United States. Sports pages in the newspapers report on particularly strong franchises, such as the Mexico City *Cruz Azul* (Blue Cross) squad.

Soccer's official Mexican name is *fútbol soccer,* to distinguish it from *fútbol americano,* another team sport played in Mexico.

American-style **football** has great fan appeal. In August 1994, *Los Vaqueros* of Dallas (the Dallas Cowboys) journeyed to Mexico City to play an exhibition game against *Los Petroleros* of Houston (the Houston Oilers). The contest drew a crowd

of 120,000 wildly screaming Mexican fans. It was the largest crowd ever to see a National Football League (NFL) game. Every Sunday during the football season, several NFL games are televised in Mexico, where they are watched by a devoted audience. Mexicans have taken a particular liking to the Cowboys. Despite the game's popularity, however, only a few Mexican high schools and colleges field American football squads. Equipment such as helmets and shoulder pads is too expensive for the budgets of most Mexican schools.

Mexican schoolchildren playing American-style football during recess

The most popular Mexican baseball star in the United States major leagues was **Fernando Valenzuela**, a native of Sonora, Mexico. In the early 1980s, Valenzuela pitched for the Los Angeles Dodgers, and he took the United States by storm. In 1981, he won both the Rookie of the Year and Cy Young awards in the National League. Fans became swept up in "Fernandomania" as the Mexican left-hander became baseball's most popular pitcher. At the same time, Fernando was a walking god in his home country of Mexico. When his games were televised in Mexico, a strange hush overwhelmed the country as fans concentrated on every pitch. In Los Angeles, Mexican-American fans brought loud mariachi bands to the ballpark and turned Dodger Stadium into a Mexican fiesta.

The country's second most popular team sport is **baseball**. The "national pastime" of the United States caught on in Latin America and in the Caribbean region in the early 1900s and remains an institution south of the U.S. border. In Mexico, the game was first played by farmhands, and several professional teams today retain names like the "Coffee Field Workers" and the "Sugar Field Workers."

Because baseball is a direct import from the United States, some of the language is the same, but some terms have been adopted in Spanish. The shortstop is called the "shortstop," but the batter is a *bateador* and the pitcher is the *pitchador*. Mexicans use the English word "base," but pronounce it the Spanish way: BAH-se.

In 1947, Jackie Robinson became the first African American to play in the U.S. major leagues, and from then on, more and more black players were signed to U.S teams. But before this, many African Americans went south of the border to play pro baseball because

Fernando Valenzuela

Safe at home!

racial barriers did not exist on Mexican teams. Today Mexican players work hard to improve their skills in the Mexican leagues, hoping some day to have a shot at the "Bigs" to the north. Mexican baseball emphasizes speed and fielding more than it does home-run power. Fans in Mexico love to watch daring baserunning and crisp double plays.

Sometimes a soccer background helps a baseball player. One splendid baserunner was Bobby Avila, who was born in Mexico and played for the Cleveland Indians in the 1950s. He was the first Mexican ballplayer to become a star in the

Bobby Avila in 1952

United States, and his baserunning style took American players by surprise. Using his soccer skills, Avila could kick the ball out of an infielder's glove as the man tried to tag Avila out. Avila was also college-educated and a gifted public speaker. After he retired from baseball, he combined his speaking skills and his baseball fame and was elected governor of the Mexican state of Veracruz.

Playground basketball in the Mexican city of Torreón

As in the United States, **basketball** is mostly a city game in Mexico. Parks in all urban areas have basketball courts. Since Mexico has mild winters, outdoor basketball is played all year long.

The country has yet to develop international stars because Mexican people tend not to be extremely tall. In 1994, the U.S.-based Continental Basketball Association established a franchise in Mexico City, but only one Mexican, a 6-foot-4 guard, made the team. The other players were all imported from the United States.

Volleyball is a team sport played with zeal in Mexico, especially by women. *Vóleibol femenil* (women's volleyball) is played at the college level and the games are given extensive space in the sports pages. Women's basketball is also followed avidly. Mexican women often complain that their society is dominated by men, and that they suffer discrimination in jobs and educational opportunities. But in team sports, women enjoy some degree of equality. Among the spectators at women's volleyball and basketball games, men cheer loudest of all.

A player for Mexico's national women's basketball team

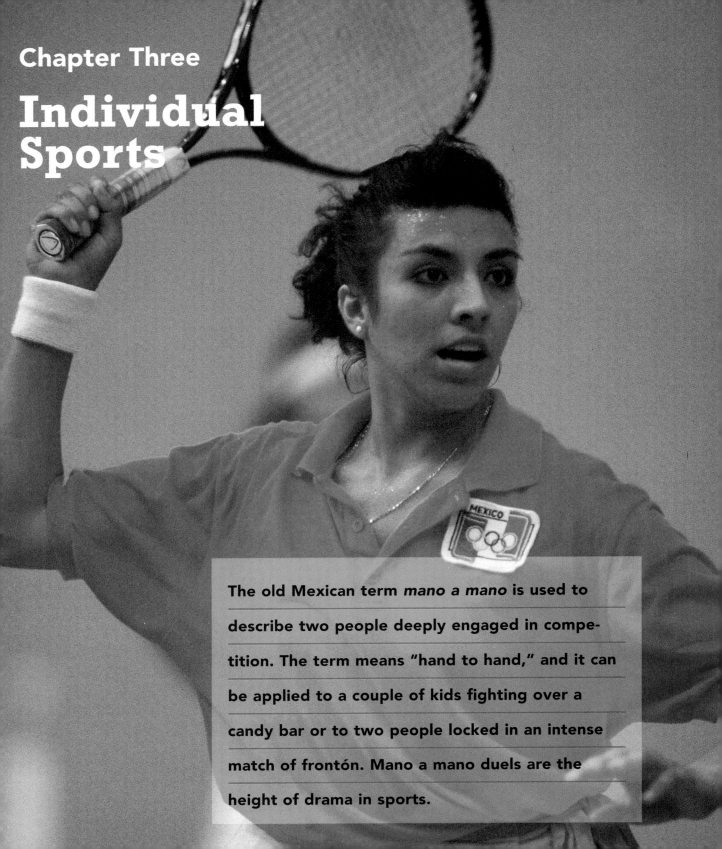

Chapter Three

Individual Sports

The old Mexican term *mano a mano* is used to describe two people deeply engaged in competition. The term means "hand to hand," and it can be applied to a couple of kids fighting over a candy bar or to two people locked in an intense match of frontón. Mano a mano duels are the height of drama in sports.

Tennis is among the most elegant of the mano a mano games. For years, tennis was a sport for rich Mexicans. Most courts were in private clubs or on the grounds of mansions. More and more public courts are opening now, which allows ordinary people to play. But tennis remains a game pursued mostly by the well-to-do. Still, the country has produced many exciting players.

In 1963, the Mexican Rafael Osuña won the United States Open, one of the most important tennis tournaments in the world. Osuña had a friend, a younger man named Raúl Ramírez, who was also destined for stardom. Ramírez was a powerful player in the 1970s, and he won many international tournaments. Also, Ramírez possessed movie-star good looks, making him a heartthrob around the world. At the height of his career, Ramírez married Maritza Sayalaro, a former Miss Universe.

Pancho González, one of the great tennis players of all time, was a Mexican American born in Los Angeles in 1928. When he wanted a bicycle, his mother refused to buy him one because she thought it was too dangerous. Instead, she bought him a used tennis racket for less than a dollar. Young Pancho knew nothing about tennis, but he started practicing by hitting an old ball against a wall. From these meager beginnings, he rose to become a well-known player even before he was a teenager. González developed into a fierce competitor. He would stalk the ball like a panther and fire it back to his opponent. He hit the big-time in 1948, when he won the U.S. Singles Championship. He continued winning championships through the 1950s and 1960s. Even in his forties, Pancho González was a top tennis performer.

21

Tennis has two "cousin games," **jai alai** and **frontón**, that are actively played in Mexico. Both games are played in three-sided courts, and both involve batting a ball against a wall.

Jai alai is considered by many experts to be the world's fastest game. It came to Mexico from the Basque region of Spain, and it is played primarily in Mexico City and in the border town of Tijuana. Players use a curved wicker basket to catch and fling a rock-hard ball against the wall. The ball travels at speeds up to one hundred miles per hour, making it difficult for the opponent to return. Within the jai alai family is the popular game called frontón. The game is played with standard tennis rackets and a tennis ball. Players bat the ball off a forward wall and keep it going until someone misses. Frontón courts are found in all Mexican cities. The game requires tennis skills and tireless devotion. Frontón matches can last many hours.

A statue of a *jai alai* player at a Tijuana jai alai court

There is a subject Mexicans talk about among themselves, but are reluctant to discuss with others. That subject is *machismo,* or *macho,* behavior. It refers to an exaggerated idea of manhood, a sort of bravado that is sometimes displayed by Mexican males. A "macho" man will never back down from a street fight, even when he is outnumbered or if his opponent is bigger and more powerful.

machismo

an exaggerated expression of manhood, bravery, or physical strength

Some historians say the macho attitude has deep roots. Five centuries ago, Spanish invaders came to Mexico and freely took pretty Aztec and other Indian women as wives and girlfriends. As a conquered people, the native Mexican men could do little to stop the Spaniards. Machismo, the historians argue, is the modern man's way of paying back that insult. But many Mexicans claim that macho behavior does not really exist in their society. They maintain that the whole image of the macho man is an unfair stereotype.

Perhaps the macho image is fueled by the Mexican love for **boxing**. The sport is popular in every corner of the country. The *Arena Coliseo,* a dingy boxing stadium in the heart of Mexico City, hosts matches four times a week. Boxing rings are often set up in the open air outside of small towns, and the fights draw thousands of fans. The devotion to boxing has translated into

A poster listing the schedule of fights at Arena Coliseo, Mexico City's main boxing arena

Mexico's boxing hero, Julio César Chávez (right), in a 1992 Mexico City bout

soaring success for Mexican fighters. Mexican boxers are ranked among the best in the world, along with African Americans and Cubans.

The country's most celebrated fighter is Julio César Chávez. His popularity is so great that, if put to a vote, he might be elected president of Mexico. Born in the northern state of Sonora in 1962, Chávez has collected more victories in the boxing ring than any other lightweight in history. He is famous for attacking opponents in a military fashion, always advancing until he traps his foe in the corner. Then his powerful right hand goes to work with the relentless fury of a piston driven by a machine.

Chávez's fans are legendary. They flock by the thousands to see him fight—even if he is fighting in the United States or in Europe! Waving Mexican flags, his followers chant out: "CHA-vez! CHA-vez! CHA-vez!" When going against this mighty lightweight, an opposing boxer does not fight only Chávez—he also fights the entire Mexican nation.

Wrestling is another popular spectator sport in Mexico. Serious wrestling matches are held in high school and college gyms and in health clubs. But, as in the United States, legitimate wrestling attracts few fans. The public prefers professional wrestling, a staged event where good guys battle bad guys while the audience boos or cheers. Spins and body throws in the pro matches are carefully rehearsed. Sometimes the contestants appear to be dancing with each other. Many wrestlers wear outrageous costumes that go along with their nicknames. The wrestler called *El Diablo Rojo* (the Red Devil) climbs into the ring dressed in a blazing red outfit equipped with a pointed tail. Pro wrestling is more sideshow than it is sport, but fans love the action and the drama. And they have fun watching the bad guy get creamed.

Chapter Four
Bullfighting

The American writer Ernest Hemingway once wrote
an entire book about the bullfights he saw while
living in Spain. He called the book *Death in the
Afternoon*. Hemingway loved the color, the music, and
the drama associated with the sport of bullfighting.

exicans are as devoted to **bullfighting** as the Spanish. The *corrida de toros* (bullfight) was brought to Mexico from Spain almost five centuries ago. Today the corrida is hailed by fans because of its pageantry and the courage and grace shown by the bullfighter. Mexico City's bull ring, the *Plaza México*, holds 50,000 people, making it the largest such arena in the world. It is filled to capacity for all major events.

corrida de toros

Spanish term meaning "fight of bulls" or "bullfighting"

An old joke is told about a tourist from the United States who loved Mexico but hated bullfighting. So he regularly went to the bullfights and cheered for the bull. Strangely, that tourist was doing exactly what the bullfighting *aficionado* (fan) does. Experienced spectators watch the bull as closely as they do the bullfighter and his assistants.

Above: Matador Teodoro Gomez

Opposite page: A father and son practice with the cape in a Mexico City park.

toro bravo

fighting bull

Bulls used for the corrida are born to battle. Comparing a *toro bravo* (fighting bull) with a bull from the farm is like comparing a tiger to a housecat. The fighting bull is bred to be fierce, fearless, and eager to kill. A bull that is weak in the ring is a disgrace to the ranch that produced it.

A bullfight unfolds in precise steps. Typically, it will start at 4:00 P.M. Usually three *matadors* (the principal bullfighters) will fight two bulls each, one animal at a time. To begin the spectacle, a band bursts into music and the three matadors lead a parade of their assistants into the arena.

Picadors on horseback enter the ring during the opening ceremonies of a Mexico City bullfight.

The matadors are dressed in tight-fitting uniforms with colorful sequins running across the seams. Their appearance is so important that they often take several hours just to get dressed!

A matador takes a long time to prepare for an afternoon in the ring. Here, Manolo Martinez (inset) prays before facing the bulls.

The parade is a prelude to a drama in four acts. To start the first act, workers swing open a gate and a huge black bull storms into the arena. Snorting and kicking, he is a thousand pounds of fighting fury. A matador's assistant, called a *banderillero,* marches out to goad the bull into charging his cape. After several charges, a trumpet blast announces the second act—the entrance of the *picador.* Mounted on horseback and armed with a

A *banderillero* jabs a bull with *banderillas.* People unfamiliar with bullfighting might think the sport is cruel, but it is a centuries-old tradition in many Hispanic cultures.

banderillero

matador's assistant who weakens the bull by stabbing it with *banderillas*

long lance, the picador rides to the center of the ring. Instinctively, the bull charges the horse, but the horse is protected by a blanket as thick as a mattress. While the bull sinks its horns into the blanket, the picador jabs his lance into the bull's shoulders. This process weakens the animal and makes it hold its head down in the final battle with the matador. Another trumpet blast signals the third act. This is the placing of the *banderillas.* These long wooden sticks have colorful decorations. But at the ends are sharp, barbed points. The three banderilleros re-enter the ring, and each, in turn, rushes up to the bull, passing perilously close to its sharp horns, and jabs two banderillas into its neck. Now all is ready for the final act, which pits the matador, alone in the ring, against the killer bull.

Matadors tend to be trim, athletic, and hand-some. They are idolized in Mexico. Posters bearing their pictures are pasted on the walls of restaurants, barbershops, and grocery stores. Little boys grow up yearning to become brave matadors. Boys will practice with one bending over, holding a pair of wooden horns at his head, and charging into the other's cape. There have been some women matadors, but bullfighting has traditionally been dominated by men.

The final duel between matador and bull lasts about twenty minutes. This period is called *la faena de la muleta* (the work of the cape). It is the dramatic climax of the corrida, the show-down that the customers have paid to see. With the grace of a dancer, the matador coaxes the bull to charge his cape. He entertains the crowd by performing cape trickery. One particularly difficult move is called "the natural." It requires the matador to stand motionless while the bull charges under his arm. The bull's sharp horns pass inches from his chest.

la faena
de la
muleta

the beginning of the final
duel between matador
and bull

A matador in the final
showdown with a bull

The object of this final stage of the battle is to control the bull, confound his senses, and set him up for the kill. When performing the kill, the matador must lean over the bull's powerful head and plunge a sword deep into its neck. A properly thrust sword will kill the animal almost instantly. If the sword is inserted incorrectly, the matador must chase after the bull and jab it again and again until it finally dies.

Is the corrida a grand event of profound beauty, or is it one of ugliness and cruelty? The debate rages on and on. Many people object to the very purpose of the sport. It is a game designed to torture and eventually kill an animal that has no choice but to fight and die. The bull ring is certainly the bloodiest arena in modern sport. Many sports fans are sickened that the slow, gory death of an innocent animal is seen as entertainment by bullfighting fans.

Defenders of the corrida point to the skill and artistry of the matador, his deft moves and his boldness. They say the bull is bred to fight and to die in the ring. Many supporters of the corrida argue that the bulls are so ferocious they hardly feel the pain from the picador's lance or the sharp banderillas.

Masters of the Corrida

Poems and songs are written honoring their courage. They are the masters of the corrida, the handful of men who are considered to be the world's greatest bullfighters. A matador named El Cordobás of Spain is a bullfighting immortal, as is Carlos Arruza of Mexico. But elderly aficionados still speak in hushed tones about Spain's Manolete. He is thought of as the greatest matador in history. A bullfighter since he was 17 years old, Manolete was the shining star of the 1930s and 1940s. He devised the *manoletina*, a cape technique named for him, in which he induced the bull to charge under his outstretched arm while he stood as still as a statue. His fights were a symphony of grace and style. Manolete died in 1947 after he was gored by a bull in a Spanish arena.

33

Chapter Five

Olympic Glory

Every four years, world attention is riveted on the Olympics, the grand festival of sports. Ideally, the Olympics highlight individual excellence among athletes, but fans most often root for the men and women who represent their own countries. Fan excitement rose to dizzying heights when the games were held in Mexico in 1968.

Never in the annals of Mexican sports was there a year like 1968, when Mexico hosted the Olympic Summer Games. It was the first time the Olympics were held in a Latin American location. Mexicans prepared feverishly for the great event. A new stadium, a swimming facility, and an entire Olympic village were constructed. The Mexico City subway, which transports people around the capital today, was built in honor of the Olympics. When digging the subway, crews unearthed many ancient statues and temples left by the Aztecs. The Olympics reawakened the Aztec relics which had been sleeping beneath the streets for more than four hundred years.

Above: The *Palacio del Deporte*, a Mexico City basketball arena, was built specifically for the 1968 Olympics.

Opposite page: Mexican boxer Ricardo Delgado shows off the gold medal he won in the 1968 Olympics.

Olympic Tragedy
In the late 1960s, political protest rocked college campuses in the United States, Europe, and in Mexico. Just days before the 1968 Olympics were scheduled to open, Mexico City police fired into a crowd of students demonstrating at a downtown plaza. Police claimed the students fired first, but the students and many eyewitnesses said the police opened fire for no apparent reason. The terrible shooting spree raged for several minutes. The government later said 49 people were killed, but observers maintain the number of dead was far higher. The "Olympic Massacre" caused bitter feelings against the government, but it did not dampen the excitement of the games.

During the two weeks of frenzied competition, Mexico enjoyed its best Olympic performance ever. Led by its boxers, Mexico won three gold medals (for first-place finishes), three silver medals (second place), and three bronze medals (third place). The country's most dramatic triumph came in the wiggly looking track-and-field event known as racewalking.

Racewalking is sometimes called heel-and-toe walking because the rules require the athlete to touch his leading heel to the ground before raising his trailing toe. A walker who breaks contact with the ground—this is called "floating"—will be disqualified by officials judging the race. In the Olympics, two racewalking contests are held—one of 20 kilometers and another of 50 kilometers. Racewalking had long been a popular sport in Europe, but before 1968, it was virtually unknown in Mexico.

It was late afternoon when the leading walkers of the 20-kilometer event approached the entrance to the Olympic Stadium. (All distance contests begin in the main stadium, then travel a route through neighboring streets, and finish with a final lap in the stadium.) As the walkers entered the stadium for the final lap, two Russians held the lead, but a Mexican was in third place. He was José Pedraza, a 31-year-old soldier. The spectators broke into a thundering chant: "*Me-xi-co! Me-xi-co! Me-xi-co!*" No one had dreamed that a Mexican would win a medal in this event.

During the stadium lap, the people watched, electrified, while Pedraza inched past the second-place Russian. Pedraza now gained on the leader as the crowd's ear-splitting chant continued: "*Me-xi-co! Me-xi-co!*" The Russian then put on a magnificent spurt to preserve the lead and the gold medal. Pedraza captured the silver medal. The race remains one of the most dramatic moments in Mexican sports history.

Pedraza's heroics began an amazing string of successes for Mexican walkers. At the

Mexico's premier racewalker, Ernesto Canto (number 99), leads the way.

Raúl González (left) and Ernesto Canto (right) carry the Mexican flag in triumph at the 1984 Olympics.

¡Me-xi-co!
¡Me-xi-co!
¡Me-xi-co!

Montreal Olympics in 1972, Mexico's Daniel Bautista won the gold medal for the 20-kilometer walk. The country's greatest triumph came in 1984, when Ernesto Canto and Raúl González won the gold and silver medals in the 20-kilometer race. Several days later, González stunned the track-and-field world by placing first in the rugged 50-kilometer race. The 1984 Olympic Games were held in Los Angeles, home to millions of people of Mexican heritage. During the walking races, Mexican Americans stood along the Los Angeles streets cheering frantically for the athletes of their mother country.

Mexico's Susana Diaz competes in an international track meet.

A Tarahumara long-
distance runner

Before the Spaniards arrived, Mexico was home to many thriving Indian civilizations. Today the *Mestizos* are the dominant group. Mestizos are people of mixed Indian and European blood-lines; pure Indians are now a minority. The Mestizos live in many regions throughout Mexico, including Oaxaca, Chiapas, Tabasco, and the Yucatán Peninsula. In the northern state of Chihuahua, some 40,000 Indians live in the wildly beautiful Copper Canyon. Along the canyon's steep banks live the Tarahumara, who might be the world's strongest **distance runners**.

For centuries, the Tarahumara were self-supporting hunters and farmers. In recent years, they began taking jobs at mines. How do they get to work in the morning? They run. No one knows why. When asked why they run to the mines, the people simply shrug their shoulders and say, "To get there."

The Tarahumara run everywhere. If they wish to visit a village some fifty miles away, they will run to it. In the old days, they hunted deer by running the animals into exhaustion. They play a game called *rarajipari,* in which two teams kick a wooden ball over a playing field that measures about one hundred miles long. An extended game of rarajipari consists of three days of almost constant running. The players break only to sleep.

Tarahumara women play a popular stickball game that involves running great distances.

For a long time, Mexican track coaches have fantasized about using the Tarahumara in international track meets such as the Olympics. There is no telling how many medals they could win in the Olympic marathon, a grueling 26-mile contest. Once, track coaches did approach Tarahumara runners and ask them to run the marathon. The Indians pondered a race of 26 miles and said, "Too short. Too short."

Many Indian cultures are disappearing in Mexico. People who used to live in isolated communities are now mixing freely with the mainstream population. Because of this trend, the Tarahumara might eventually be mixed completely into Mestizo society. If that happens, nobody will ever know how these fantastic runners would fare in the "too short" marathon.

Mestizos

people of mixed Indian and European bloodlines

Chapter Six

Games of the People

Organized sports are played in gymnasiums or on clearly defined fields. But many other sports and games are played on sidewalks, in homes, and on beaches. These are the games of the people. They are spontaneous bursts of pure fun and are often livelier than organized sports.

Click...click...click. This is the sound of dominoes being tossed on a table, a sound heard throughout Mexico. At home, children learn dominoes as soon as they know how to count. Neighborhood kids get together in groups and play dominoes amid shouts and giggles, much the way young people in the United States enjoy video games.

Dominoes originated in China and was introduced to Europe in the 18th century. Spaniards eventually brought the game to Mexico. When played seriously—as it is in Mexico—dominoes demands great mathematical and memory skills. A player must always know which pieces are already on the table and calculate combinations that are likely to appear next. This is the only way to block an opponent and to preserve one's own "run." To be a dominoes champion requires the power of deep concentration.

The click...click...click of dominoes in a town square

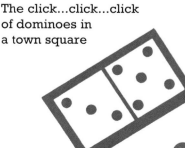

Elementary-school girls playing jump rope during recess

¡Baila Josefina, como una gelatina!

Sidewalk games played by kids call for little concentration. They are explosions of pure joy. **Jump rope** is the most popular sidewalk game in Mexico, especially among girls. While skipping rope, girls chant songs with words that rhyme but make little sense. One such song refers to Pancho Villa, a famous general in the Mexican Revolution of 1910–20: *"Pancho Villa, le gusta la tortilla, con pan y mantequilla."* Translated, this means: "Pancho Villa, likes the tortilla, with bread and butter." Certainly this is gibberish, but who cares? The words are fun to sing, and they rhyme. Another jump-rope song goes: *"Baila Josefina, como una gelatina."* This means: "Dance Josefina, like a bowl of Jello."

An ancient sidewalk game still played in Mexico is the **sea serpent**, or *la vibora*. To play, children form a line, one behind the other, with their hands on each other's shoulders. Linked together like this, they look like a long sea serpent (or snake). At the start, the whole chain passes under a "bridge" made by two children who hold hands at about shoulder level. The kids in the line sing: "*La vibora, vibora de la mar, todos quieren a pasar.*" ("The serpent, serpent of the sea, all want to pass.") On the last note, the two children making the bridge bring their hands down sharply, and those who are cut off at the back end of the serpent are eliminated from the game. No one knows the origin of la vibora. Children learn it from their parents, who learned it from their parents, and so on. The sea serpent is the Mexican equivalent of "London Bridge Is Falling Down."

la vibora
sea serpent

The popular Mexican game of sea serpent is very similar to the game "London Bridge."

A young girl takes her swings at a piñata.

piñata

the favorite Mexican party game

The most famous of all Mexican party games is the breaking of the **piñata**. A piñata is a papier mâché figure of an animal or geometric shape. The figure is brightly painted or is covered with decorative paper. Hidden inside is a ceramic pot full of treats, such as candy, fruit, and toys. A party guest breaks the piñata with a stick, and then the other children swarm in to pick up the goodies that fall to the ground. Seems simple enough, right?

But wait. The child with the stick is blindfolded, and the piñata hangs from a rope that is swung like the pendulum of a clock. Tradition demands that little kids get the first turns to break the piñata, but they usually lack the strength to do the job. As more children take their swings, the excitement of piñata is stretched out, often for an entire hour.

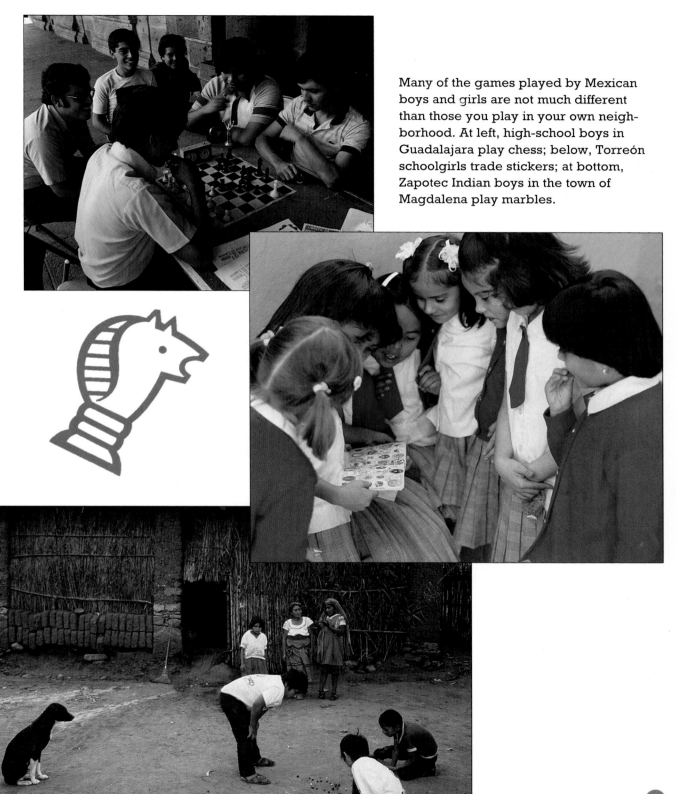

Many of the games played by Mexican boys and girls are not much different than those you play in your own neighborhood. At left, high-school boys in Guadalajara play chess; below, Torreón schoolgirls trade stickers; at bottom, Zapotec Indian boys in the town of Magdalena play marbles.

How Can I Play?

You Will Need:
- a small clay flowerpot (can be purchased for less than a dollar at most garden stores)
- individually wrapped candy or miniature candy bars
- aluminum foil
- strong wire or a few wire clothes hangers
- about ten feet of heavy string or rope
- strong tape (packing tape)
- cardboard
- papier-mâché
- crepe paper
- paints and paintbrushes

The old Mexican custom of breaking a piñata will have your friends buzzing with excitement at your next birthday party. But piñatas can be hard to find in stores in the United States, so you'll have to make your own. Making a piñata is almost as much fun as breaking it. But it can be a messy task, so you should first get your parents' permission and work in the basement or your back yard.

Piñatas come in many sizes, and they look like many different kinds of animals and shapes. The piñata described on the next page will look like a *burro*, or mule.

4. Smear papier-mâché over your entire piñata. While the papier-mâché is still wet, stick on bits of crepe paper. Or, if you wish to paint your piñata, wait until the papier-mâché dries. Be creative! Use lots of colors!

How to Make Your Piñata

1. Fill the flowerpot with candy.

2. Seal off the top of the flowerpot with aluminum foil. Wrap a band of strong wire around the center of the flowerpot and twist it so there is a hook at the other end. The flowerpot will form the burro's body.

3. Tie the string or rope to the hook, and suspend the pot from a tree branch in your back yard. Using coat hangers or strong wire, create your burro's tail, neck, and four legs. Wrap cardboard and tape around the legs, neck, and tail to make them firm and thick. Then attach these limbs to the flowerpot with tape.

5. Now create your burro's head—you could use a balloon or a large grapefruit.

49

If it isn't too cold, a waterfall can be great fun!

The long and narrow country of Mexico has more than six thousand miles of coastline. Mexico is bordered by the Pacific Ocean to the west, the Gulf of Mexico to the east, and the Caribbean Sea to the southeast. These lovely expanses of seashore make the nation a swimmer's paradise. Beach resorts, such as Acapulco on the Pacific, and Cancún on the Caribbean, are treasured spots to water-loving tourists.

But the vast majority of Mexican people live in the mountain regions, far from the sea. The inland population, especially the poor people, almost never see the oceans. **Swimming** is therefore a regional skill in Mexico. Children who live along the coasts start swimming in lagoons almost before they learn to walk. But kids in Mexico City or in Guadalajara might never learn how to swim at all. There are swimming pools in the cities, but most of them charge an admission price that a poor child cannot afford to pay.

A Mexican family at play in the local swimming pool

Mexican diver Cristina Millan
flies through the air

Diving holds a special place in the hearts of Mexicans. Some of the world's best competitive divers are from Mexico. But **cliff diving** is the passion of people who live in the beach resort of Acapulco. Along a rocky cove called La Quebrada, divers have thrilled tourists for years by plunging gracefully off the tops of cliffs. In the air, they spread their arms like the wings of a bird. At twilight, they dive holding two flaming torches, and the orange flames arc like Roman candles into the sea. Like bullfighters, the La Quebrada divers are heroes to coastal Mexican children. Boys and girls aspiring to be divers practice by leaping off low cliffs from a group of islands near Acapulco's luxury hotels.

At La Quebrada, a diver takes a good, long look (above) before his dramatic and dangerous dive into the sea below (left).

Diving is a dangerous way to make a living, and the only pay comes from tourists who hand out tips for especially stunning performances. Still, the divers take pride in their work. While soaring from La Quebrada's cliffs, they execute an exquisite dance that ends in the sea below.

Chapter Seven

Mexican-American Athletes

A quick survey of just two popular

U.S. sports—golf and football—

reveals the contributions of many

sons and daughters of Mexico.

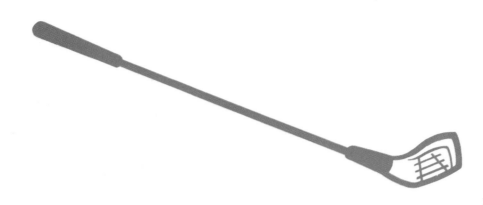

T hink of the early American colonists, and the image of the Pilgrims comes automatically to mind. But a decade before the Pilgrims landed at Plymouth, Mexican people founded Santa Fe, now the capital of New Mexico. Mexican pioneers also established Albuquerque, San Antonio, Tucson, and Los Angeles. Today more than 15 million people of Mexican descent live in the United States. From early times, Mexican Americans have enriched the United States in the arts, in business, in politics, and, of course, in sports.

The world of professional golf is serious. Grim-faced men and women study a putt as if their lives depend on the shot. During an important game, many players do not speak a word, let alone crack a smile. And then there is **Lee Trevino.** At the height of a tense game, Trevino will wander toward the crowd and wisecrack with fans. Or perhaps he'll clown with his club, using it as if it were a pool cue.

Above: Lee Trevino

Opposite page:
Nancy Lopez-Knight

Lee Trevino coaxes a putt into the hole.

Trevino was born outside Dallas, Texas, to an impoverished Mexican-American family. He was picking cotton in fields before he was ten years old. All his Mexican-American neighbors went to the fields to work at young ages. In high school, one of his jobs was cutting grass at a golf course. There he began to practice, and by the late 1960s, he entered the world of professional golf. In 1971, he was the first golfer to win the U.S., Canadian, and British Open Tournaments. *Sports Illustrated* named him Sportsman of the Year. Today he is a popular golf commentator on television, and he is one of the most popular players on the senior golf tour. Trevino has a loyal band of fans who follow him so closely they call themselves "Lee's Fleas."

Another Mexican-American golf star is **Nancy Lopez-Knight,** who was born in southern California and grew up in New Mexico. Among the world's top women players, she started in the game by accompanying her father to the golf course and practicing with a shortened club. By the time she was 11, she was beating her dad. In 1979, she was named Pro Golf Player of the Year.

During the 1980s, Lopez declined to enter many tournaments in order to spend time with her children. She remained golf's strongest advocate of women's participation. "I'm really excited about the large number of women who have taken up the game," she said. Like Trevino she urges players—both men and women—to enjoy the game instead of pulling their hair out over a missed putt. She says, "I do not understand people who approach a round of golf as if it were a death march. Relax. Lighten up." Nancy Lopez-Knight also has her special group of devoted fans; they are called "Nancy's Navy."

Nancy Lopez-Knight is one of the most accomplished golfers in the history of the sport.

Tom Flores takes a victory ride after his Los Angeles Raiders won Super Bowl XVIII.

Tom Flores labored as an NFL quarterback for ten years. He lacked the powerful arm needed to loft a long pass. He also did not have the speed to escape rushing linemen. Still, he won games because he possessed an intangible element essential to all winning quarterbacks— leadership. When facing a critical third down situation, his calm instructions in the huddle inspired his teammates to succeed. It was no surprise when Tom Flores became an NFL coach shortly after he retired as a player.

Flores was born in Fresno, California, to a humble farm family. His father had fled Mexico during the bloody revolution of 1910–20. Throughout grade school and high school, Tom worked side by side with his family, picking fruit on southern California farms. Certainly the Flores family were underdogs by U.S. standards. And it was in the role of the underdog, in 1981, that head coach Tom Flores led the Oakland Raiders into Super Bowl XV. Winning three road playoff games, the Raiders were the first wild-card team to make it to the Super Bowl. And in the big game, Flores's team ousted the Philadelphia Eagles, 27-10. Three years later, Flores and his Raiders (now playing out of Los Angeles) scored another Super Bowl upset by trouncing the Washington Redskins, 38-9.

During his stretch of championship seasons, Flores relied on **Jim Plunkett** to quarterback the Raiders. Plunkett is of Mexican-American, German, and Irish heritage. He was born in San Jose, California. Both his mother and father were blind. Plunkett attended the prestigious Stanford University, where he won the coveted Heisman Trophy in 1970. He enjoyed less success as a pro, and was on the verge of quitting football when Flores urged him to join the Raiders. Flores admired Plunkett's intelligence and, above all, his leadership ability. Flores was proven correct when Jim Plunkett threw three touchdown passes in the 1981 Super Bowl and was named MVP of the game. Plunkett repaid the California communities he played for by becoming a career and life counselor for Hispanic youth.

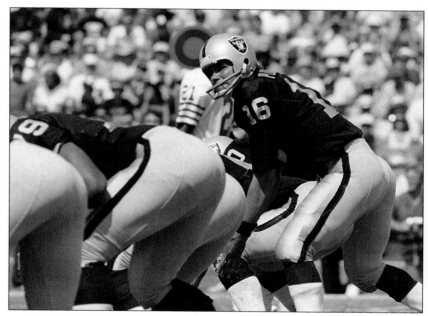

Raiders quarterback Jim Plunkett calls out the signals.

Glossary

aficionado
the Spanish word for "fan," as in "sports fan"

Arena Coliseo
the main boxing stadium in Mexico City

Aztec
Indian empire of Mexico that thrived for centuries (from about A.D. 1200 to 1500) before arrival of Spaniards from Europe

banderillas
long wooden sticks with barbed ends used to stab a bull in a bullfight

banderillero
matador's assistant who stabs bull with banderilla

corrida de toros
Spanish term for "bullfight"

la faena de la muleta
final period of a bull fight, in which the matador uses his cape to coax the bull into charging

frontón
a game similar to tennis and jai alai in which players hit a ball with a racket off a high wall

fútbol
Spanish word for "soccer"

fútbol Americano
Spanish term for American-style football

jai alai
a game similar to tennis in which players catch a hard rubber ball in a wicker basket and hurl it against a wall

lance
sharp spear attached to the end of a long pole; used in bullfighting by a picador to stab a bull

machismo (or macho)
Spanish term referring to an exaggerated or overblown male attitude of physical strength or power

mano a mano
Spanish term meaning "hand to hand"; used to describe two people in competition with each other

manoletina
a cape move used by the legendary Spanish bullfighter, Manolete

matador
Spanish term for "bullfighter"

Maya
Indian culture of southern Mexico that thrived for centuries (from about A.D. 250 to 800) before the arrival of Spaniards from Europe

Olympic Games
tournaments held every four years in the winter and summer in which nations' athletes compete against one another; Mexico City hosted the Olympic Summer Games in 1968

overtime
an extra period of play in team sports such as soccer and American football

picador
a horseman in a bullfight whose purpose is to weaken the bull by stabbing it through the shoulder muscles with a long lance

pickup game
informal team game in which players simply arrive and choose teams

piñata
children's party game in which blindfolded players attempt to break a hanging papier mâché figure with a stick

Plaza Mexico
the main bull-fighting ring in Mexico City

racewalking
Olympic track-and-field sport in which athletes race while walking heel-to-toe

rarajipari
game played by the Tarahumara Indians, in which players run while kicking a wooden ball over an extremely long field

shootout
a final period of play that decides the winner of a soccer game if the score is tied after overtime

soccer
word used mainly in the United States for fútbol, the most popular team sport in the world

tlatchtli
Aztec game that resembled a combination of today's soccer and basketball

toro bravo
a bull that is bred and raised specifically to be used in bullfights

la vibora
"sea serpent"—a sidewalk game played by Mexican children

World Cup
soccer tournament between national teams to determine the world champion; held every four years in a different host country

ndex

About the Author

R. Conrad Stein was born in Chicago. After serving in the Marine Corps, he attended the University of Illinois and received a degree in history. He has written many other books for young readers for Childrens Press and other publishers. Mr. Stein lives in Chicago with his wife and their daughter, Janna.

Mexico has long been a second home for the Stein family. Janna has spent every summer since age five in the town of San Miguel de Allende, Mexico. Her best friends are Mexican children. She grew up speaking Spanish, and many times, she experienced the joy of sidewalk games such as *la vibora de la mar*. Janna Stein can be seen playing *piñata* at a Mexican friend's birthday party on page 49 of this book.